Likabehandl

Sweden Considered

in Verse

A Toast to the Future With a Glass of Cyanide

BY THE SAME AUTHOR

Poetry
Makers and Destroyers
Surveying the Wreckage
The Belt Room
Love's Troublesome Journey
The Sex Doctor
Curriculum for Excellence
Queens of the Reich
Scotland's Saint
Wrong Ticket Home
Let's Go Ahead, Then!
Epiphany in Azure: Columba on Iona

Biography
William Wallace
Robert the Bruce
Janet: A Life in Verse

Poetry coming soon
The Best Shovel for Concrete and Sand
Banzai!: Facing my Enemies
Relentless: The Death March to Educational Excellence

Likabehandlingsplan

Glenn Telfer

Certain that someone out there likes this stuff.

Published By
Big Ride
6/3 Pinkhill Park
Edinburgh EH12 7FA
Scotland

A catalogue record for this book is available
from the British Library.

ISBN: 978-1-909297-28-9

Cover by Glenn Telfer

Design by Wordsense Ltd, Edinburgh

Printed by Charlesworth Press, Wakefield, Yorkshire

CONTENTS

	Page
Likabehandlingsplan	1
Living the Dream	3
Living the Dream	5
Gudinna i Kaffeverket	8
Pure Malt	9
Gallus	13
A Hardy Race	15
Gårdagens Make	17
Titti and Fanny	18
Flygande Tefat	20
Adventures on the Tunnelbana	21
Sex Tunnelbane Hallplatser	23
Eye Contact	24
On the Autistic Spectrum	27
Four Seasons in Two Minutes	29
Algebra	31
The Night Watch	33
Packing a Chib	36
Almost Like Stealing	37
Normal 8 Years Olds	40
Stormakstiden	41
Is this not worth fighting for?	43
The Gas Chamber of Guilt	45
Dignity of Office triptych	48
The Man-boy of Education	51
The Power Girls	53
5th Century Rome	55

Leonardo's Dream diptych   57
The Crossing Police   61
Stormakstiden   62

Notes   65

Likabehandlingsplan

Treat everyone the same way
a fine idea, the aspiration
to assuage our guilt for something
we're not exactly sure what

can go too far when
respect is extended to fruit.
T-bana passengers packed tight as
crated bananas on their trip here

one breaks free from the press
and finds a seat to itself
sitting pretty and conspicuously
yellow and silent like the other

passengers show typical consideration
for its feelings and let it be
looking at it and waiting for it
to be claimed or (more likely?) to get off.

I'm hoping, one tiring of extreme politeness,
will say, 'Excuse me, is that seat taken?'
So I can say, 'Are you blind, Man.
Can ye no see the banana sitting there?'

Är du blind, Gosse!

Kan du inte se att bananen sitter där?

Living the Dream

Leva Drömmen

Living the Dream

I remember still the thoughts
on being invited into Zoe's
bright green garden playhouse
for afternoon tea;

jealous that she had her own house,
and delighted that her kindness
extended to an invitation
– her previously ignoring me.

I was the charmed object
of all her precocious hostess skills
as homemade soup, triangular
sandwiches (so she claimed)

tea and buns were plied on me;
refusals of refills not accepted.
That the service and comestibles
were plastic mattered not one bit.

And in those endless minutes
(actually about twenty) before
she tired of me I clearly and
strongly wished that I could live

just like this forever
in this perfect little house.
Be careful what you wish for
as it may come true

often said as a warning
in my case completely ignored
as I was six years old, however
the principle still holds.

And then, fate being a noted joker,
the wish comes true fully
fifty years later the reality
not so delightful at adult scale

and minus basic services,
previously not considered
as important in that first trial
of domestic life.

I realise now, obliged by the mad
lottery that is Stockholm's housing
situation, to accept a 6sq m red
and yellow child's garden playhouse

as my (hopefully) temporary home that the wish was a
mistake.

A feeling compounded as
bending low to enter through
the little tomte sized door
a sudden epiphany, on seeing

Zoe's face again in my mind's eye,
that her invite was not the trial marriage
I was hoping for, she was just
using me to practise her hostess skills

for someone more important.

Current address:

Roda tomte lekhus,
Varingevagen,
Kungens Kurva,
Stockholm.

Gudinna i Kaffeverket

Aplomb, her *pas de bourrée*
appreciate, especially, that *derrière*
like a gift from a god

to this goddess here
with the perfect *cambré*
and my heart melts at

her look upon me, gentle,
benevolent, controlled,
en ballon, slightly too satisfied

with her own beauty and
its acknowledgement seen
in my eyes of her power

over me and others who
also watch perhaps too
struck with the irony

of her serving those
who would serve her
at the very least, irresistible

she glances at me *temps lié*
writing this, smiles sweetly,
knowing it is about her.

Pure Malt

'Over the mountains, over the main.
Through Gibraltar, to France and Spain.'

Under a lilac evening sky
a kilted sporraned braw laddie
manned the bass guitar
chords thumped like cannon
manly voices in tartan
jumped into the fray.

Then bagpipes; in the still air
the music swept all before it
like the charge of grapeshot
mentioned in the song. Although
without the carnage
to the French. Images came

thick and fast, Killiecrankie,
Bonnie Dundee, the '45.
Jacobites and their claymores
1812, the Peninsular Wars,
French hussars, the sabre cut
that ruins the face forever.

Kilted Scotch ay fighting
basket hilted for their prince
red jacketed for England
(although really for pride)
with musket, and inevitably, bayonet
defying any to stand before them.

And yet this
get a kilt aroun yer knees
was no Jacobites gaitherin,
but a charming café
set in a lovely bay
in peaceful Sweden

the band astonishingly
totally Swedish
the audience Swedish too and,
as expected, mannerly.
The bevvying, restrained,
except for us.

Bagpipes and martial music
combined with drink
heated the blood,
and as the bottles
piled up I became
my own recruiting sergeant

so ready was I
for the King's Shilling.
So sign on bonnie laddie
An cam awa wi me.
With those of a certain pedigree
the mood was evidently catching.

'Now I feel like a fight,'
said my son, reaching
and gripping the neck
of yet another bottle
as if it was the hilt
of his claymore.

I thought of ancestors.
Not with irony
or false sadness for men
I did not know.
But with a strange understanding
that the music had imparted.

My kilted grandfather
7435462 Cameronians
ruined by gas, his brother
lost forever in the Somme.
The box of jangling medals
that I loved as a child.

There was drink involved!

But I was no maudlin drunk
ignorant of the other truth
behind the crash of the guns
and the medals' bright shine.
Pride and grief: different sides
of the same coin.

At the interval in conversation
with the highlanders' leader,
'Why sing of my country's past?'
Who wants to sing about
progressive social policies?
And who wants to hear it?

But you are so lucky in Scotland
to have such a marvellous history
and the greatest music

to celebrate it. That is why
my heart is a Scotsman.
And I am out for the '45.

And then,
standing before a foreigner
who had felt from a distance
the magic in what
was mine all along,
a gigantic pride filled me

bubbling up from my feet
like it had been
poured into me
from a jug
Aye, I thought. Aye!
'Gimme the pen, I'll list up!'

Gallus

That swaggering walk grabbed my eye
the unmistakable stamp of my city
Glasgow abroad here in Stockholm

a ba' hair over 5' 3", the perfect expression
of my city's genetic genius for miniaturization,
the better to fit ten to a room

he saw me looking and looked
straight back directly holding
the gaze, *I'm thinking he's thinking*...

before nodding a friendly
Ho there, Big Man, instead of a
Whit are you looking at?

Chest thrust forward to the world
as if to barge through the crowd
to the bar counter

arms swept back hinged at the shoulder
slightly proud of the hips as if packing
although not today, and here, surely?

His standing-still posture was so
ridiculously suggestive of the Square Go
that I was almost tempted to challenge

as a joke, which I knew he would
understand as such, and return the same
immediately, *Let's go ahead, then!*

Which, if I had, would have been
a mistake and a surprise both
big hoor size

as I realized just as my train pulled away
that his gallus posture on the platform
was not an accident of birth and

rearin up in my toun, but
an accident! him packing not a chib
but a plastic arm poorly fitted

although maybe the real one was chopped aff
in a gang fight with samurai swords
in a Stockholm milk bar;

mibbe aye, mibbe naw.

A hardy race inured to cold

I'm dressed for summer
shorts and t-shirt at 7:10am
early November air temperature
seems right for me who ay runs hot;
probably manopause!

Passing my colleagues on the road
jacketed up, scarfed, gloved
and hatted, as if in a different land,
Do you not feel the cold?
One asked, reminding me it is winter.

Barely zero, I genuinely didn't
and the thought occurred of
all those hardy warriors
of my race scorning sleet
hail and empty stomachs alike

all night marches in all weather
followed by a pre-breakfast battle
were never a problem, indeed,
a speciality!
And me wondering

all those years I read of this
where they had gone,
my ancestors? Uncomplaining
and bare-arsed
famous for their spirit

in cold weather and light-heart
in heavy circumstances.
And then the answering smile
of recognition now that I know.
That's me!

Gårdagens Make

He was a bit dried out looking
as you would be too
if you had sat around
for a whole day under glass

waiting, forlornly, as it happened
on someone wanting you
which, when you want them to,
they never do.

The day started fresh and hope
was high, the contents excellent
and much experience went
into the presentation

but sometimes you don't meet
the one, it's not a fault
it's just how life is and
you're left on the shelf.

At half price my parsimony
considered him, but the
epicure defeated the miser
and I went fresher.

What happens if no-one wants him?
I take him home, she said.
For yourself? *Sometimes.*
And sometimes I feed him to the dog.

Titti and Fanny

Fulfilling a long held ambition
to find myself stuck between
that perfect pairing

on seeing the gap open I knew
I'd have to dive in quick before
some knob spoiled it for me

as across the room I read
the same intention in the eyes
of Renaud, that crafty Frenchman.

Collocations that match up
with secretion lubricated
my slide into that lovely location

as at last (and about time!)
I was getting some (so to speak!).
They noticed my shit-eating grin

simultaneously bemused, they asked
Why are you smiling so big?
I couldn't possibly explain and

… keep my job. *Oh, nothing,..*
I've just had a happy thought and
I've always wanted to sit next to you ladies.

They looked at each other quizzically.
Puzzled as the inscrutability of foreigners
once again hid the dirty mind.

It's a dream cum true.

Flygande Tefat

Aliens wishing to preserve
the Earth for future colonization
rejected the nuclear option
for something slower;
attacking the dentition

they being a patient life form
and fond of a joke creating
the marketing opportunity
among gullible Earthlings
by a few promo flights
around US airbases and
Bonnybridge, Scotland

and then manufactured
miniature versions of their
interplanetary craft with
a front company using rice
paper and sugar instead
of atomic fusion composites
and bio-nano technology.

The colours however are authentic
for they know where to draw the
line with humour.

That the product is made in Belgium
is just a coincidence.

Adventures on the Tunnelbana

Äventyr på Tunnelbanan

Sex Tunnelbane Hallplatser

Mariatorget
Two nice-looking birds
with two muppets
like Abba and then

Zinkensdamn
one nice-looking bird
with two muppets.

Hornstull
One nice-looking bird
with a guy who
sounds like a muppet.

Liljeholmen
Three muppets and no
nice-looking birds

Aspudden
then no birds at all,
nor any muppets.

Örnsberg
Finally, a nice-looking bird
with no muppets,
unless you count me.

Eye Contact

a Jacobite exile, he would have you believe,
at 6.22am on the Tunnelbana, but
missing a sporran *and* chib (although
sporting other waist-bound Batman-like
paraphernalia), he's no Scotsman and

ignores my friendly stare, perhaps
suspecting I'm a Hanoverian spy.
Which I actually am, sort of.

Col. Gadaffi is not dead at all
as he can be seen
funding a comeback Scud fund
by trying to sell hats and gloves
from a holdall at 6.26am

to Kim Jong 11 naturally dwarfed
by an incognito (no cape) Thor looking
conspicuously white within a herd

of large African dictators, all eyes
down having lost their mojo
along with their Swiss accounts.
And, this being Sweden, two Muppets,
two Hobbits and an Orc.

Check out at 6.28am
Big Mamma Cass matching in poundage
any dictator you care to mention

and what appears to be,
judging by her haughty expression,
The Queen of Sheba, and
some Chinese acrobats inscrutably
sitting under their own Beijing Cirkus poster,

then a thuggish looking geezer,
Quick, look away!...
Oh, that's my reflection!

Silent, this enclosed world of samtals
keeping in touch at 6.31am.
to the empty air, intently focussed
on their life as lived apparently
trapped in a little thing

that demands worship and obedience
to the portable shrine of the jealous god,
of themselves

jealous like a drug.
No-one catching an eye for actual contact;
perhaps, this art already, like fire-lighting
with sticks, forgotten.
I note the focus on playlist and status update

brings no pleasure to the eye
while mine lights with recognition of home
I had no idea that Rangers made a rucsac

or how it travelled from its lair to here:
here being the back of a wee wifie
wi a dug in a shopping bag.
Only the dug looks at me
at 6.34am.

On the Autistic Spectrum

One end; let's take Glasgow toun
Saturday night, anytime after 10pm
pishing up alleys, bawling the odds
selfies wi flashed knickers, beer can
spiked on railings

the Duke traffic coned again
feral manic ganged-up and out there
How ur ye daein, Big Man?
Careful, he's not actually asking
what he's asking!

I easily read the interaction
the threatening manner is
a greeting in that language
and we part as best mates;
How to make friends-Glasgow style.

Now slide down the scale

Other end; Stockholm, tunnelbana.
Any day, any time you like.
Middle aged lady, in pink ribbons
her fanny licker dog.
Opposing seat, another passenger

another dog, mongrel, no ribbons.
They sniff each other up
and make friends easily while
the respective owners stare
out of the window.

Finally, mongrel owner copies
the doggy template and tries a foray
into language, *She is so pretty!*
Yes, she is. End of conversation.
How to make friends-Stockholm style.

Hon är så söt.

Absolut.

Four Seasons
in Two Minutes

The presence of a banana
seems to instantly bring
on summer's beaming face

just as instantly as angry autumn
arrives with the crop's last bite,
there is the tiniest gap,

this is early October,
while fresh supplies are expected
then hoped for and when

disappointment is confirmed,
at the season's end, the dark
clouds of winter scud in.

These are angry clouds, noisy
and wet, but spring arrives
in the middle of a winter storm

as she catches my eye and notes
I hold her stare unafraid
of the girnin or how she might

involve me in her problem;
curiosity trumping anger.
Spring's uncertain clouds part

revealing summer's bright smile
which returned naturally
creates a lovely June evening

between us, the gloaming
lasting between stops
and still present in gold

as the door closes leaving
me on the platform and her
on the train with autumn

imminent as it moves away.

Algebra

Never judge a book by its cover
the reverse equation equally true;
Never judge a cover by its book.

Here we have a perfect example
mathematically perfect, *id est*,
of the principle

large carrier bag of discarded cans
and bottles, a pant collector,
to be converted

in another mathematical certainty
to other cans and bottles
in his chosen tipple

by his habit I'd estimate
superlager, aquavit
or primus stove fuel

and then I check the book
I see his lips synching,
Algebraic Equations.

Deep in that precise world
of life's only proven truths
as he followed the steps

equalizing the equation
and perhaps, on paper at least,
his life itself

an unbalanced x= me
an unsolvable differential
in the span allowed for proof

a whole life working
on a private Fermat until
degree by tiny degree

driven to distraction by y
or x2 he jumped the rails
and onto the page

of a parallel life where sober
equals drunk and the hobo
existence some sort of solution

which for us all is
just one bastard
integer away.

The Night Watch

Wearing the uniform, or whatever...

Neither bold nor wary
public guardians going in threes
the better to take good
care of themselves

chewing gum, texting, chatting
foot up against the door
lout style, the *esprit de corps*
of our night watch officers

making the infamous
Bold Gendarmes almost
seem like bold gendarmes
these neds with dirty boots,

pepper spray, stab-proof vests,
on public money doing
nothing but representing
the principle far in excess

of public safety, their purported
and pretended purpose, when
spotting some real louts
(MENA, *surprised?*) getting on

they suddenly collectively
needed a mocha and pastry
and made a dash for the
platform, the doors closing on

so staggeringly a bold display
of cowardice that it becomes
an incentive to behave bad
for those in two minds about it,

which our new fellow travellers
instantly confirm never were
anyway, taking stylistic cues
from the degenerate template

provided at commune expense.
What public purpose is served
by this perfect expression of less
than useless you might think;

but then the realisation
of the diabolical genius in
the social vision built of
self-hatred and anomie contained

in the tableau viewed as the train
pulled away, one at the booth
ordering the coffees, the other
busy texting and the last

stretched out on a bench, no doubt
exhausted from various forms
of loafing, already ear-phoned and
all utterly invisible to the public

except as a too visible
manifestation of the surrender
of public space to those who would
want it for sport and mischief

but policing in full measure
the guilt found in the quotas
and ticking all the boxes back
at the station at shift's end

in harmony to the internal hysteria
of the country as it gives itself away
in a kind of collective suicide
but being Sweden, ever so quietly.

Meanwhile, for us incarcerated
for another stop, the louts
upped the ante in the game
of 'stop me if you dare' and for

protection I imagined another watch
and see Captain Cocq stepping
out of the painting:
I'll show the Zweeds how it's done.

Arquebusiers, prepare your pieces.
Pikemen, follow me…
Gentlemen, let us restore our good name.
Fellow Citizens, be not alarmed!

Packing a Chib

Daily they are to be seen
packing a chib, carrying
in full view of who's looking

unconcerned
about knife searches
or scaring the public

on the subway this morning
enough steel was on view
to carve a subway map

of Glasgow on the faces
of the whole Fleet or
of yer Tongs (Ya bass!)

But such tools need the workmen,
if such they are called,
and here there are none.

No chance of *the* question,
Whit the f… ur yoo lookin at?
where every possible answer is wrong.

And with that realisation,
the other; that
the real chib's in the eyes.

Almost Like Stealing: 1

Nature's Bounty

Rhubarb blueberries pears and
at least two types of apples
precision timed just for me,
asking to be made into a crumble

which I did and then ate
now done and all gone
an embarrassingly profligate
bounty which

cost not a bawbee and
hardly an ounce of effort-
bar the collecting.
All the while thinking,

Is this what the Garden of Eden felt like?

Feeling unworthy of the gift
and thus awaiting the punishment
in lieu of payment
knowing its coming anyway.

Eve just anticipated the future.

Almost like Stealing: 2

The Cancer Express

He makes his way up the carriage
handing out printed leaflets.
I can read them easily
they're in English, except for 'Tack.'

I refuse it and he blanks me
handing it to my neighbour
and I read it just the same
his wife has' bad cancer' (so it says)

and there's her picture
in happier times with
their three sons all still home,
location unlocated, waiting…

If only the Swedes could help?

He comes back minutes later, collects
his leaflets and cancer op funds; zero kronor
accepted with impressive equanimity.
I saw the same leaflet last night;

The cancer woman's husband, a completely different fellow.

Almost like Stealing: 3

Tableau Vivant with Antiope and Pit Bull

She is unquestionably attractive
in an edgy, 'Here Comes Trouble' way
and a slightly different me
would have given her the money,

although not for that!
Her pit bull, a vicious fashion accessory;
this girl could tear the face off you
which is why the passengers

put money in the paper cup, fear
a better social leverage then pity.
She looks as grateful as her dog
eyes as cold as the coins,

What sort of little girl's life led you to this?

Strong arming on the tunnelbana
a planet of the apes 'boyfriend' nearby.
Step away from this anti life
the strong horse you need for escape

is across the platform, the carriage doors already open for
you.

Normal 8 Year Olds

Seemingly chartered for pupils
who are elective mutes and
apparently invisible to each other,
this carriage

en route to the quiet Bedlam
of their school, only grouped
together because of the strength
in their vicinity

of the WiFi signal, finding
the focus on task previously
reserved for something
called playing.

Come on, look up and smile.

Stormakstiden

The Great Days

Is this not worth fighting for?

Freyja, her name.
The etymology is fascinating
and somewhat complex.
The idea is simple;

she is beautiful, blue-eyed,
slightly remote, golden sun turned
to perfect female form.
Obviously, her hair is braided.

She parts the clouds
in a fairy tale
(Take this from me)
Ta detta från mig.

Her hand sweeps over the land
'Du gamla, du fria!'
It is ancient, but fresh, clean.
This land is my body

treat it with respect, love it
and it will pay you in kind.
(Is this not worth fighting for?)
Är icke detta att värt försvara?

Then time grows tired.
The arm grows weak,
then weaker again,
the spirit lost in shopping

Freyja see what is happening,
Loki's handiwork,
has infected the maidens
who now worship at his

temple of chaos.
The last 1000 years were a test
to be worthy of the gift
and finding not, she steps away

flames howl after her, rubble
fills the chosen nightmare
Loki takes off his mask and smiles.
Too late the offer of everything

under the gun's iron eye.

The Gas Chamber of Guilt

As if,

they chose association by preference
and, one must assume,
Volk und Blud.

Hobby too, might explain with some
their otherwise extreme choice
of summer vacation

in the ultimate (literally)
holiday camp as volunteers
for the kinder

their kindly manner
and simpleton expressions
facilitating compliance

with the final solution
to their charges' problem;
ethnicity.

You can imagine their shock
when it was revealed that
this well-intentioned good deed

has shifted from the credit
to the debt column in the ledger book
of world opinion. *Nej, fan!*

But how to atone for the guilt
with a people not given
to public displays of anything

was the question
in every Swedish mind
and then an answer

from the brilliant F1 minds
of Sweden's famous feminists
of both genders (as it then was);

Identify the country's guilt
with men and make them
pay in kind (and then some)

for their patriarchy,
Folkblod spilled and fire
delivered by importing

the world's greatest levellers
from Barbary, the Levant, Kush
and the Horn

who go to work with evident
relish and professionalism,
Walpurgis now forever

only a moment away!
Is this enough to lift the stigmata;
purge our rayciss self by fire

and outbreeding?
Our children's future in hell
to top trump the guilt?

As if,

Dignity of Office Triptych

Swedish Culture, Bah!

The nation's fame rests
on its arts to travel the world
as ambassadors,

as befits its self perception,
Sweden turns its back
on its bloody Viking inheritance

of edda and skald to embrace
introspective poetry, angst
theatre and, as balance,

jolly fiddle and dance
yellow and blue folkdräkt
this is gentle fare, apparently.

But hiding its true face
under the schnapps and
handclapping at Midsommar.

Sweden's Shame, Bah!

The minister's embarrassment
must have been acute
at the ambassador's party

when the Ferrero Rochers were
handed out and comparisons
made to the stunning

cultural achievements of
the New Swedes' old homelands;
witch burning, tribal assassinations

(always in colourful robes!)
the fiddle and foot stomp
of harvest in happy village greens

a poor second place to the vibrant
music of massed AKs celebrating
the end of lippy females.

Reputation Restored, Bah!

More than most, our minister of culture
(she was an officer of state after all)
knew that justice provoking

whiteness lay like a snake
beneath the rustic charm
of Old Sweden's cultural traditions.

Time to do her job
and cut off the snake's head
bring Swedish culture up to date;

the dignity of office demanded it!
Luckily, her MTV education
provided the template and showed

Sweden's new face to the world,
by getting her tits out for the boys
– and any other grateful genders.

Beat that Norway!

PS. Request from His Majesty, Carl XV1 Gustaf,
to his ministers: Keep your breasts inside your
blouse while on government business.

The Man-boy of Education

A tribute to Gustav Fridolin

He's a government minister
although I think he's 12 years old
puberty's on the horizon
he twits and tweets a lot.

His ideas for education
are framed around virtues
common to his peer group
of, as they fancy it, rebels

fighting for justice, tolerance,
the enrichment of public
education via multiculturalism;
ideas they have invented!

His life is digital and so he sends
out his leadership messages
from his bedroom via Youtube.
Fair enough, he's too young to work.

Standards aren't plummeting
if you hold the graph upsidedown.
The circle is square and life is good.
Here's a little heart sign, *Love you!*

Because he respects the job they do
when he grows up
he wants to be a teacher;
a punishment most condign.

Bet he won't be!

The Power Girls

Having waged a successful war
of the scorched earth variety
the power girls of the apocalypse
take the citadel and smash the ceiling.

These girls, for such they are
even at 40 +, posing for selfies,
high fiving each other
gratulating for their own success.

And here's me as the
Minister for Defence.
OMG, I can't believe it. That is
So Amazing! You go girlllz

as women sticking it to the men
in the heart of the manosphere
in what was formerly the sacred
duty of the menfolk, protect

your kith and kin and borders
against enemies and traitors;
just the sort of sexist idea you
would expect from the patriarchy.

So Manist! Time to show the
world what defence is really about
put this house in order and start
by sweeping out the guns.

The military's new job, the girls tell us,
is to defend, not their countries, but
the quotas. Go full social justice
the bullet budget better spent:

Transgender Specialist: Recruiting Now.
The iron hand of Mars
now a powder poof
the army's strong focus now

on gluten free, purple hair dye
and pride days for ethnic diversity
medals shine for gender tolerance
as a fairer way to defend

our thousand year reich
a construct which has had its day.
Driving Scandinavia fast to its tomb
the girls pause only to tweet LOL.

5th Century Rome

This active and indomitable race, being excited by an
unrestrainable desire of plundering the possessions of
others, went on ravaging and slaughtering all the nations in
their neighbourhoods until they reached...Sweden.

You'd think it would be a singular thing
for a whole country to commit suicide
by inviting in people who would
happily set your car on fire

and rape your children! What sort
of hopium were Swedes taking when
they decided to become a 'humanitarian
super-power'(©1966) and Save the World,

what source the hubris that infected
that ingrate generation who frame
their virtues around no sacrifice or
service of their own, although

in the fullness of time they will pay
more than their fees for studying
gender instead of the Bible, mighty
Gibben, and failing even a passing

acquaintance with the Khalifs of Baghdad.
We imagined the future we would make
like a big happy café seen in a movie,
all the world was there discussing

as equals, our unhappy histories
all forgotten as we share recipes;
Your meat curries really are the
dog's bollocks. Thanks for that enrichment!

Hammered into young brains every
single day for 50 years; diversity, enrichment,
responsibility, guilt, requirement, deception
hypocrisy…diversity, enrichment…

bump bump bump, the steady drumbeat
of rhythm that kills and now the pace
picking up as Sweden burns to
the deafening crescendo of sirens;

when it stops that's when you worry.
It stops! And the head clears of endorphins
you step out of the café into
a colder northern Mogadishu.

Vem fan är alla dessa cunts?

Leonardo's Dream diptych

The Dream

in the dream as in real life
the pupil kicks off as usual
in the dream Leonardo presses a button
and within a minute the HT arrives

he's a big guy, more bouncer,
than therapist. Actually,
not therapist at all!
Problem?, he asks. Leonard points.

HT packs a taser and pepper spray
approaching said lout he holds
them up, *Leave now or choose one.*
The pupil is huckled out. Amazingly,

with none of his customary lip.
End of problem, lesson proceeds
like a lesson should. Smiling kids.
Class actually happy; really!

HT comes to see Leonardo later
tells him that the parents called
to complain. HT gives them it, boss style;
No-one messes with my staff.

Your kids barred for the week.
Sort him out or don't bring him back.
Gee, Leonardo says, **Thanks, HT.**
Don't mention it. You're a great teacher

and I'm calling time up for ingrates.
Anyway, I was wanting to try the taser
...maybe next week? And...
don't worry, Leonardo, I've got your back.

Then the bell rings and
a new period starts...
Actually, it was the alarm clock
for a new day.

The Reality

in real life as in the dream
the pupil kicks off as usual
in real life there is no button to press
and no-one arrives to rescue the class

after half an hour of torturing
the teacher with comic questions,
pretend sleeping and snoring,
earthquake sneezes in which he

falls off the chair and feigns
an injury, spills water, breaks pencils
(twice), 'accidently' hits another pupil
and otherwise ruins the lesson

to great comic effect with his
select audience of neddish morons,
he leaves to go to the toilet
without asking or returning.

Later, HT sends Leonardo an e-mail:
Come to my office, 12.30 pm.
Leonardo arrives and sees said
lout inside enjoying chat with HT, laughing,

probably at me, Leonardo feels.
Kid actually sitting in HT's chair
while Leonardo waits for 15 minutes
like **he's** the naughty boy.

Eventually, after a high five
the new best mates part and
Leonardo enters and **not** offered a seat.
HT tells him the kid has formally complained.

We (ie, you) need to go easy on him
or they'll be trouble, maybe lawyers too.
You need to apologise, smooth things.
The bell rings for the start of a new period.

Only Jesus has Leonardo's back

The Crossing Police

Bullying children's minds by regulations
and regimenting their behaviour
in a masculine way!!!

Making sexism and Nazi-ism acceptable
by providing a little service to better
disguise what they really do.

Their understated uniforms a strong proof
by the weakest of denials
that they're the uniformed branch of **them**

who formerly wore the trousers.
For 70 years, hiding in full view these
little Gestapo men and their Quisling molls

In steps courage without limit
and forensic skills in abundance
of The Justice Warriors

their attention to truth
unmasks the ugly reality behind
every little thing.

By reality, we mean patriarchy and fascism.

There hasn't been one accident since
the crossing police started 70 years ago.
Yea, but what's your point, you sexist pig?

Stormakstiden

Gustavus Adolphus, the warrior king
defending the Prostestant faith
and making Sweden the bad boy
in the German playground

by stonking victories over
serious players in the game
of death, 17th Century style.
Big history, us Swedes matching it.

Hence Stormakstiden, our big time.
In the queen's chamber
at Drottningsholm, her palace,
a note of lament in the guide's voice

for these storming glory days
seemed like a little prayer for
a return to when truth
came out of The Bible

and campaigns for justice
were delivered by
musket, pike and cuirassier.
But these days are gone now,

Dessa dagar är borta nu,
never to return, as Sweden
takes the pacifist role forever.
I recall her words clearly

from 20 years ago.
She was a history graduate,
so she told us, but ignorant
of history's big wheel turning

and the role of infinite jest
in human affairs.
The enemy regroup, the little prayer
has been answered with a curse.

Their skirmishers are already among us.
Their torches on the horizon.
Be a Swede again, it's Stormakstiden,
there is no pacifist role.

Many blondes will be lost.

NOTES

Likabehandlingsplan: The word almost suggests in English the intention behind this Swedish state guideline for all interactions from the personal to the international; handle everyone alike. It goes beyond, I think, common decency and equality under the law, as it segues into intolerance and offence at perceived infractions of the same. Paradoxically, then, this most civic of aspirations, by way of obliging self-censorship and legitimising sensitivity and complaint, has become a dis-civic force empowering much of the 'equality and fairness' madness that has undone Sweden. The incident in the poem really happened.

Pure Malt: This is the name of the band. They are excellent.

Gallus: For those who know that stance, no further description is necessary. For the lave, here goes; a half hostile-half ironic facial expression. Shoulders back, chest out, arms hang loose at the sides. Posture alert for a sudden bottle attack, or a nice burd.

Titti and Fanny: There were actually two Fannys working there, although that would have been too much to hope for. Of course, there were scores of the usual fannies working there as well, but that's a different thing entirely.

Flygande Tefat: After a 50 years' absence, this pointless mock confectionary landed (attacked?) en masse in my local ICA foodstore.

The Night Watch: Stockholm's underground now has (needs) patrolling three 'man' security teams. They are worse than useless. Referencing Rembrandt's painting of the same and The Bold Gendarmes by Offenbach.

Packing a Chib: It used to be a commonplace to see men openly carrying a knife, and particularly workmen. Now that Swedes have imported people who actually will stab you this practice has (like topless bathing) suddenly disappeared. An alas for both.

The Gas Chamber of Guilt: The source of Swedish guilt has at last been found; Eve (of Garden of Eden infamy) was definitely Swedish, and Swedish women today keep up that tradition of ignoring anything a man (and God is a man) would ask them to do. And too, at a midsommarfest cannibalism was accidently invented when they ran out of surströmming, but not aquavit. Kannibalism, en annan svensk första!

The Power Girls: As of writing all the Scandinavian Defence Ministers are women. That's fine, of course, who should care? But, at a joint meeting, there was something not right in their satisfaction *as women* and indifferent to the fact that they don't know an M16 from an F16. *So…?* And now, to save budgets for real priorities, *dobbeltbevæpning* is required. The idea of a weapon for every soldier now regarded as a Manist idea. They'll still be sorting out the new gender bathroom arrangements as the enemy kick in the gates. Of course, as pacifists what the Swedes really want is to be defeated; their current strategy is perfect.

Leonardo's Dream/ Leonardo's Reality: A true story.

The Crossing Police: A Swedish institution that saw older children in school acting as road crossing guides and general pavement chaperones to their younger schoolmates. They usually wore a little tabard and enjoyed some privileges as recompense. In keeping with the spirit of our age, these have been disbanded.

Stormakstiden: The Swedes love this part of their history. 'I used to be a contender, don't you know.'; it's the nearest they come to boasting out loud.

ALSO AVAILABLE

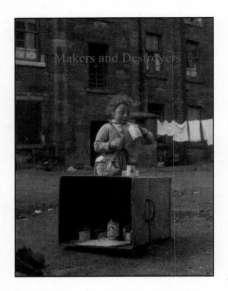

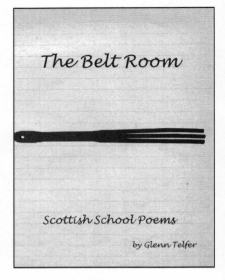

Makers and Destroyers

Glasgow; what's gone? The author examines the hammers and tongs, coal-fired world that was replaced and improved by what's came.

Or maybe not. We need a judge and jury on this; I bagsy the judge, yous can be the jury.

The Belt Room

A cross-my-heart true collection about some more-than-average tough schools during the '60s. It especially considers the use of corporal punishment (the belt) as a standard pedagogic technique; the author is well qualified to comment.

See other Big Ride titles at www. glenntelfer.me